The Bright Room

Acknowledgements

I thank the following publications where versions of these poems were first published: *Agenda, Light in the Darkness Anthology, Live Canon Anthology 2014, Poetry Ireland Review, Orbis, Poetry Salzburg, Queens Quarterly, Ontario, Sentinel, Stride, The North, The Northern Poetry Workshop Anthology: In Your Own Time* and *The SHOp.*

Thanks also to those in the poetry community who have supported me over the years. Especially Ann and Peter Sansom at The Poetry Business, Sean O'Brien and members of The Northern Poetry Workshop, John Whale and members of the Leeds University Workshop.

The Bright Room
Michael McCarthy

smith|doorstop

Published 2018 by
Smith|Doorstop books
The Poetry Business
Campo House
54 Campo Lane
Sheffield S1 2EG
www.poetrybusiness.co.uk

ISBN 978-1-912196-15-9

British Library Cataloguing-in-Publication Data.
A catalogue record for this book is available from the
British Library.

Designed & Typeset by Utter
Printed and bound by CPI Group (UK) Ltd, Croydon, CR0 4YY
Cover image: 'Skellig Michael' by Donagh Carey
Author photo: Michelle Neville

Smith|Doorstop is a member of Inpress,
www.inpressbooks.co.uk. Distributed by NBN International,
Airport Business Centre, 10 Thornbury Road Plymouth PL 6 7PP.

The Poetry Business receives financial support from
Arts Council England

Supported by
ARTS COUNCIL
ENGLAND

Contents

There are many rooms in my Father's house.

– John 14:2

The Holly Field

There was no holly in it much, though
there was a holly tree, if you could call it that.
An old stump of a thing half strangled with ivy,
the few scrawny branches with barely a leaf on them
and never any berries, not even at Christmas.

What there was, was a sycamore tree
with a fork low enough to climb up on.
You could hide behind its leaves with their
five fingers, and pretend you weren't there.

You could make it into a horse, or a sailing ship.
You'd gallop him off down the fields as far as
the river and after he had a fine long drink
you'd jump across without falling off.

You'd sail around the world and watch
the different countries as they went past,
and after you got back, you'd climb down
and run in home for a drink of thick milk
before your mother put it in a cake.

But the best thing about the holly field
was the Corncrake. You'd hardly ever
see them because they hid in the high grass,
but they said 'corn-crake' all day long until
they got hoarse, and carried on long after
you were sent to bed while it was still bright.

When the time came for cutting the hay
they'd go all quiet. The horse pulled
the mowing blade up and down the field,
and when it came to the very last sward

they'd all fly out in a sudden whoosh
almost forgetting their legs. There was
no telling where they went next.

Grandmother

My Grandmother's feet hurt, so she bathed them
in a big white bowl. My mother says it was all
the walking she used to do, over Mount Gabriel
down to Schull, then back up the mountain road.

She pulled her black shawl around her shoulders
then lifted up her black cloak as far as her ankles
and lowered her feet into the warm soapy water.
My father said: 'mo-leir, that'll soften them out'.

Her feet were like the marble altar rails at Mass.
Blotchy white, only not smooth. They were bony
like the knuckles on her wrists. My mother says
she minded me as a baby when herself got sick.

I can't remember if she had big feet but I think so.
My mother's feet were big, but they weren't bony
and they didn't hurt. When a telegram came saying
my grandmother was dead, my mother cried.

Tommy Spooney

We see him walking in the distance ahead of us
on the straight road towards Cullinagh bridge.
His black overcoat almost reaches the ground.
His white hair sprouts over the turned up collar.
His arms swing, his steps are short and quick.

When we ride past him in the horse and trap
he stands to attention and clicks his heels
and salutes my father, soldier to soldier.
My father does nothing, just cracks the whip.
The wars they fought were opposing wars.

Seven cows with their udders slack after milking
graze in the field on the hillside. Inside the ditch
there is no grazing, only rushes and bog cotton,
and thistles with red collars like altar boys at Mass.
The ditch is covered in stalks of fairy thimbles.

He doesn't live anywhere. Sometimes he sleeps
in a *bohán* surrounded by briars outside the town.
We see him receding in the distance behind us
as we rumble over the humped-back bridge.
There the horse decides to dump some dung.

The crows descend and start to pick at it.
When Tommy gets that far they'll scatter
and perch on a tree, waiting until he's gone.
He'll stop and take in the warm smell of dung.
As soon as he sets off they'll start up again.

The road now is wider than back then.
The hump on the bridge is long gone.
There are crows but no longer any dung.
The river is dredged, the bog planted.
I see him there every time I pass.

The Station Mass

First there's the preparing. The smell of creosote and lime
As they paint the shed and whitewash the house.
Then the scrubbing and polishing, and getting
The silver and the good china out of the Chiffonier,
Mary Jerry Connie coming with her butter pads
Softening it up and rolling it into little balls
The grooves from the pads stay on the butter like writing.

And then the Mass Box arriving and the men setting it up
On the table with the artificial legs Mickey Ireland made
So it would be the right height. On the morning, neighbours
On horses and carts, on bikes, or walking. The Priest
In a motor car, taken to the parlour, and people lining up
By the front door for confessions, some saying their prayers,
Others whispering at the back until their turn comes.

The Mass itself is a blur. Afterwards,
The old people talking about times past. The men
Drinking bottles of stout, and the women sipping
Glasses of sherry. And the older lads above
In the hayshed caffling and getting into mischief.
No one knows how the horse gets into the grain-loft.
But the door is wide open, and there he is

Feeding on oats like it's his birthday, until
Suddenly a hind leg goes through the floor.
He must have got a terrible fright, the ground
Giving way like that, but now he's flat on his belly,
His forelegs stretched in front of him, one hind leg
Trapped underneath him, and the other one
Minding its own business below in the stable.

Every time he tries to move, a cascade of oats
Flows onto the cobbled floor. Someone puts a sheet
To gather the grain. Someone else wraps a bag
Around his leg so he won't cut himself. His leg
Twitches but mostly it is still: the hoof in mid-air,
The pastern slim as a ballet dancer, and a shine
On his shin as the beads of sweat roll off it.

You can hear the men's voices from above:
'Never mind who let him in, how do we get him out
Without doing more harm.' 'Is there a pulley?
Will that beam take the weight? Get some ropes?'
'Out of the way or ye'll frighten the horse,' Miah Neill says.
And like a fool I run in home to tell them the latest.
Aunt Jo has the women on their knees giving out the Rosary.

'Kneel down,' she orders me, and there's no escape.
The Agony in the Garden. The Scourging at the Pillar.
Hail Marys and the Holy Marys go on and on, as the five
Sorrowful mysteries run their course. Then the glorious ones.
'The second Glorious Mystery, the Ascension into Heaven.'
I can picture the horse suspended from the roof. I can almost
Hear the men grunting as they pull on the rope.

I notice Aunt Jo saying her prayers with her eyes closed,
and before I know it I'm out the door and gone.
But it's too late. The horse is in the field,
Picking at the grass as if nothing happened.
The men are gathered in a cluster by the stable.
Grains stay imbedded in the cobbles for months.
Mickey Ireland comes next day to repair the floor.

The Rabbit

You found him below in the garden, hiding under the stone steps.
He was very small, just like the one on the silver three-penny-bit.
His back was rounded, his head tucked in and his ears standing up.
The pads of his feet were cool when they touched your finger tips.

You brought him inside so the magpies wouldn't pick his eyes out.
You fed him blades of grass and cabbage, but he wasn't hungry.
You cut up some hay and made a bed for him in the big kettle.
You put the cabbage in with him in case he got hungry later on.

Padraig Scartha a man of the roads came to the house that night.
He wore a black hat like a crow, and carried a blackthorn stick.
After the supper your father said: 'show Padraig your rabbit.'
Padraig rubbed him on his back. The rabbit didn't like that.

You put him back in his kettle before going off up to bed.
You put the kettle behind the small door, under the stairs.
It was nice and dark in there, 'like in a burrow' you said.
Padraig Scartha slept in the kitchen, on the settle bed.

When you woke in the morning, Scartha was gone.
When you looked in the kettle, the rabbit was dead.

Cyril

First there is the reaping. The horses: Bob and the Grey Mare
pull the reaper. Your father drives. Cyril's brother D.J. sits
on the side-seat and operates the reaping gear. With his rake
he guides the corn against the blade. His foot on the pedal
keeps the crate upright. When the sheave is the right size
he releases it so it slides off as the ground moves away.

Then there is the binding. Catch a fistful of cut corn
just below the grain. Twist it once, then split the straw
two ways with your thumbs, and hug it round the sheave.
Pull the ends tight, twist, then tuck the twist inside itself.
The barley's whiskers scratch your arms, mind the thistles.
Move it out of the way now and get on to the next one quick.

Next comes the stooking. Your job is drawing the sheaves.
Cyril is tall and slanted like the oats. He takes two sheaves
and bangs their heads together so they'll hold each other up.
Four sheaves each side and one at both ends to block the wind.
They stretch out in straight lines down the length of the field.
Almost dark now and the dew falling. Soon it will be done.

On Sunday night he arrives on his bicycle scoraiocting.
There's a bag of apples hanging from the handlebars.
Big broad cookers, juicy red eaters, the sound of apples
in his voice. Sitting by the Range he lights a Woodbine.
The Tilley throws his smoking shadow on the far wall.
'Bless us and save us,' it says, and the stories begin.

'Sit over here now so,' your mother says as she pours the tea.
Cyril spills his into the saucer, blows on it until it's cooled.
He lowers his head to the saucer, his hand trembles as he
lifts it to the level of his lips and takes a good long slurp.
'It was the time of the snaring of the rabbits,' he says.
Or else: 'It was the time of the skinning of the calves.'

Tell the Truth and Shame the Devil

Whenever mud was found on the stairs, or a handle
Knocked off of a cup. Or the gate of the haggard
Not closed and the cows getting into the spuds.
Or the hen house door left open all night for the fox.

How in-the-name-a-God did the horse get into the loft?
Who was it drove the wrong sow into the farrowing pin?
Who ate a hole out of the bottom of the Christmas cake
Before it was cut? Come now, tell the truth and shame the devil.

✳

He bought them out of a half-crown Peter Brien gave him.
I saw the bulge in his pocket where he hung his coat.
My hand brushed against it by accident, I heard a rustle.
I was trying to find out what it was when a toffee fell out.
I was trying to put it back when it slipped into my mouth.
It tasted like honey from the combs my uncle found
In the cornfield, where the scythe had cut off the top.
I tried another to see if it tasted the same, and it did.
So I tried one more, and then one more after that.

It wasn't stealing. I gave some to my other brother
To see what he made of them. He said they were nice.
So I couldn't have been stealing, and I didn't tell a lie.
I examined my tongue in the looking glass and there was
No sign of a black spot. I told the truth and shamed the devil.
But my brother said the only devil I shamed was myself.

Autumn

Autumn almost didn't happen this year.
For a long time it was somewhere else.
Waiting in line behind a summer which
failed to appear. I made holes in the carpet
so the mice wouldn't have to, seeing as
there was no bread and hardly any crumbs.

Crumbs was the lie I told my mother
that first time autumn nearly didn't come.
That was the year I hung out the washing
on the barbed wire fence around the hen coop.
'To frighten the fox,' I said, when she asked why
I'd done such a silly thing. But it wasn't all that silly.
There wasn't much chance the washing would blow away.
And no chance at all the fox would steal my sister's blue blouse,
or go running off in my uncle's Long Johns, the ones that needed mending.

The Mounds

A day off has been declared and this group,
short of money or friends, have stayed behind.
They sit on the mounds and watch the world as it
refuses to go past. Harte is holding a blade of grass
between his thumbs. Sullivan is showing him how
to make it sing. Sullivan can make the note of a thrush,
Harte makes the broken-winded wheeze of an old horse.

O'Shea is brushing his crew-cut, persuading it
into a *duck's ass*. Flynn has a hurley and sliotar.
He asks if anyone is up for a slog. The Dean
Sammy White, appears at the door in his soutane.
He walks up and down twice, disappears again.
Riordan, propped up on his elbow is taking it all in.
O'Shea picks up his hurley and says: 'come on so.'

Stuffing their trouser legs into their socks
they climb under the wire and onto the pitch.
Flynn is a concrete block, all muscle and grit,
O'Shea is a sally rod, with a sweet clear stroke.
Low and hard, back and forth, forth and back,
the slap of ash on leather alternating with grunts.
After ten minutes O'Shea lobs one into the air.

Flynn doubles on it, sends it higher, and shouts
'Sputnik Two.' They keep at it, high as they can,
until they reach the count: 'Sputnik fifty seven.'
The world as they know it will eventually pass.
Riordan will watch Telly with his grown up kids.
Who wants to be a millionaire? The question:
the name of the first space craft to orbit the earth?

'Sputnik,' he'll say. '1957.' No need to phone a friend.
They'll wonder how he's so well up on space travel.
He'll think of Sullivan, and Harte trying to whistle
with a blade of grass. O'Shea with his trousers loose
and his shoes all scuffed. Flynn with his shirt soaked,
his forehead beaded, the pungent smell of his sweat.
And under his own elbow, the feel of the earth.

Newton's First Law of Motion

When a thing is going it stays going.
And when a thing is stopped
It stays stopped.

Westerns

The Lone Ranger started me off when I was seven. First thing
Home from school I'd read his comic strip in the Cork Examiner,
To see if he'd captured the outlaws, or got himself out of a scrape.
One time, his gun-belt gone, his hands tied behind his back
They were going to take his mask off. I was frightened for him.

But Silver galloped off to find Tonto, and they got there in time.
Years later I went to see him at the Pavilion on Patrick Street.
He had an American twang. I felt betrayed. It was worse than
Losing his mask. I thought his accent was the same as mine.
I lost interest after that, but I still watched and read Westerns.

I loved the long rides in the prairies, nights under the cold stars,
Shoot-outs. Zane Gray: *Riders of the Purple Sage*. My favourite was
Louis L'Amour. The sound of his name, and the titles of his books:
High Lonesome, Down the Long Hills, Showdown at Yellow Butte.
I loved being in them. I'd swap them with Steve, the fastest gun alive.

Westerns are not on my mind the summer I fly out to Colorado.
I want to be in the wild. I drive west from Pueblo, raft on the river
Then on to Ouray and over the San Juan Skyway. I pull in at Snake Pass
Pick a wildflower: Indian Paint Brush, Columbine, for each person I love.
I pull in to Durango at dusk, stop at a Motel with 'John Wayne slept here.'

I happen on the Louis L'Amour Saloon. His rocking chair is out front
Beside a rack of his books. My eye lands on *The Man from Skibbereen*.
Fancy a Western called after my home town. A quick browse tells me
It's not very good. He just liked the name. Tomorrow I'll head south
To Mesa Verde, but tonight I'll step inside and be a cowboy again.

His website shows he died that year, but nobody in Durango was aware.
A hundred books all still in print, more than three hundred million sold,
A multi book deal with Bantam, thirty years on and still being turned out.
Last summer I met Steve again, in a wheelchair now and home from Texas.
'What was it we liked about Westerns?' I ask him. 'The scenery,' he says.

Saivnose

Nobody, not even the Master, was sure what the name stood for,
only that it rose east near Carrigfadda – meaning the long rock,
and flowed into the Ilen at Bauravilla below Dereeney Bridge.

It was not a big river as rivers go, but it was big enough.
Once, long before our time, a girl had drowned in it.
She slipped off stepping stones near Breadagh Cross.

On summer evenings around dusk you could watch the fish
leap the Drominidy falls where, after dark, night after night
Jerome Jerry Connie and friends were too quick for the bailiffs.

A net across the bottom, and a few stones thrown in at the top
left them with a nicely collection of brown trout, their taste
all the nicer by the way they were caught.

From the northern inch across from Mickey Ireland's cottage
down as far as the waterworks and the footbridge we crossed
on our way to school was the stretch that I knew best.

In winter the line of rusted ferns and mulch left on the fields
marked how far the flood had come out. The winter before last
was as high as I'd ever seen it. My brother says he saw it worse.

In summer when the water was low the gravel gathered in a heap
in the middle, you could see the shine on the stones like amethyst,
and under the brow the banks had a black beard of withered moss.

My uncle swam at Poll Na Guella after he came home from China.
He read his breviary in the shade of a furze bush. I swim here now.
I leave my breviary at home, and dive straight in.

Something Happened

'Something happened to them,' she'd say if they were back late
or if it got dark and there was still no sign of them, especially if
they were at the races. She'd start getting restless – doors opening
and closing – then put on her coat over the blue apron and go outside.
She'd walk north to the stable and milk churns, south to the turf rick.
You'd hear her anxious exhaled prayers over the hedge: 'Jesus Mercy.'

'Go up to the cross', she'd say 'like a good boy, and see if there's any
trace of them' or 'go east to Dan's, maybe they've heard something.'
And you'd go up the road in the dark, as far as the cabbage garden.
You'd slow down when you came to the corner near the spot
– in case he was there and wanted to say something – though you knew
he wouldn't, because he was in heaven. Still, you could never be sure.

So you'd wait a bit, then take a deep breath and run, making a noise
so everything else was drowned out. Then you'd stand at the cross
look north and south, and you'd know there was no fear of them.
Nothing ever happened again. There were the usual falls off bikes,
damaged elbows, broken wrists, cut knees, but nothing like that.
As we grew up things improved. Not that she ever got over it.

Forgotten Hermitage

You sit relaxed, leaning back, your head resting against
A boulder. You look down over the rock-scape to the ocean
And the lighthouse, taking it all in as you let the breeze
Feather your face and neck. You absorb the moment,
Feel the calmness spread along your body.

Your breathing steady, it comes to you if you're ever
To climb to the southern peak the time is now. Without
Hesitating you walk gingerly along the narrow ledge
Until you reach the chimney. You look to the sky, not
To the ocean seven hundred feet below, and you begin.

Gathering yourself into a crouch, with muscles tensed
You place one foot into the first step, wedge yourself
With your back to the rock and begin the ascent.
You pull yourself up step by cut step, until you
Emerge through the open space at the top.

You stand upright, take deep breaths, look out over
The western world. In a while you sit next to where
The water indent is scooped out of the rock. They didn't
Have much room up here. Calmness continues to bless you
As you re-imagine their life. Best not to think of your descent.

Ahiohill Churchyard

I went to see Paddy Keoghane this afternoon.
The rain was lashing down. 'I'm getting wet here,'
I said, 'I won't stay long.' 'We often got a lot wetter
playing golf,' he said; which is all very well for him.

He seemed in good form enough, his usual self,
full of chatter and wanting to know what's up.
I mentioned Man. United weren't doing too well.
He let that one pass. I asked him if he'd seen Forde.

He said he had. Forde was settling in well, staying
behind the scenes as usual, pretending he wasn't there.
'Welcome Martin, I said to him the morning he arrived.
He told me keep my voice down, he didn't want any fuss.

Harney on the other hand is mixing in with the best.
He got promoted the other week, named the Celebrant
at High Mass, he's now arranging the rota. Forde thinks
the way he's shaping up he'll go all the way to the top.'

By this time the rain had started to soak around my neck.
'Your golf hasn't improved much,' he said, 'if anything
it's got worse, and while you're at it, tell Mc Gillicuddy
there's no need to quote me every time he lines up a putt'.

'I'll have to go,' I said, the rain dreeping down my spine.
'Do you remember the day we played Halifax?' He asked.
Out on Ogden Moor, that par three 17th with the green
a hundred feet below, you'd think you could spit on it.

We got a fair wetting that day. When we came back
you soaked in the bath and John A had a hot whiskey.
Afterwards we had steaks at Ye Olde Raggalds Inn.
'Look,' I said, 'if I get any wetter I'll be joining you

and I'm not ready for that yet.' 'Right-o so,' he says
'and thanks for coming.' Going out the gate I thought
I heard him shout 'fore', but I was only imagining it.
When I turned back I banged my head on the gate.

'Look where you're going,' was the last thing he said,
'and mind yourself.' I could feel the blood running
into my eyes. His sister Catherine saw to the cut.
That's in case anybody thinks I made all this up.

A Funeral

Arriving early, knowing nothing about the dead man I find
The Church is closed. A parishioner who happens to be passing
Arranges to unlock the doors. The hearse pulls up. As we process in
Six women from the Care Home appear. I beckon them to the front,
Then place the Christian symbols on the coffin.

A Crucifix: The Book of the Gospels: I point to the Paschal Candle,
I bless his remains with Holy Water. I read from Job: *This I know,*
That my Redeemer lives ... after my awaking He will set me close,
And from my flesh I will look on God. My eyes will gaze on him
And find him not aloof.

All I know about his belief is that he had asked to have
A Catholic funeral. I invite the women to gather round the coffin,
I ask them to tell me about him. He had lived in Goole all his life,
Looked after his parents, had never married. He was a very
Private man. He had been with them for more than ten years.

He loved sport, especially football. His eyes would light up as
He told them how a game was won, or the foibles of the manager.
He watched the Olympics flat out. He was forever doing his crosswords.
Shepherd's Pie was his very favourite food. Her voice cracked at that.
A lump gathers in my throat as I pray for his eternal rest.

Last Rites

Friday evening and I finish late.
I fix myself supper: a turkey sandwich,
French Onion soup slowly warming up.
The doorbell rings, insistent and shrill.

There's a woman, smelling of horse-sweat,
her face white. Is this the Catholic Church?
Her father has been in a flying accident.
Please could I give him the last rites?

Turning off the gas I get in the car.
I follow her in her four wheel drive.
The man at the flying club tells us how
the plane banked, he didn't have a chance.

He takes us to the far end of the airfield
where the circle of scorched stubble
holds all that is left, the buckled frame,
the charred wings, but no human remains.

May angels lead you into the bosom of Abraham
and where Lazarus is poor no longer, may you
have eternal rest. Hail Mary full of grace ...
... now and at the hour of our death.

She's handed me her mobile
so her sister down south can hear.
Fragmented prayers mixed with sobs
Come tumbling from Exeter into my ear.

Later, drinking black coffee she talks
about her dad, how he loved his flying.
She was doing the horses when she heard.
It's much later when I re-heat the soup.

Margaret

She is outside pouring milk for the cat when I arrive
And despite her poor eyesight she doesn't spill a drop.
In the front room we sit on her matching green chairs,
Facing us her wedding photograph and the Sacred Heart.

Her offertory envelope is ready on the table. I ask about
Her week. She's ok, she's never been one for taking pills.
The cataracts are bothering her, the magnifying glass helps.
We proceed with the prayers and I give her Holy Communion.

When Wilfred Owen wrote his Anthem, her father wrote
From the trenches. She shows me the card he sent her, 1917
Decorated on the front, and on the back Margaret Kavanagh.
Born the month after Vera Lynn, and still bright as a shilling.

As she follows me out I see the cat has polished off the milk.
Next up are the birds. She's got the packet of seeds with her.
There's this spade lying face up farther back in the garden.
You haven't been digging again, I ask. Not yet, she says.

Taking Communion to Jennifer

I find her in good form.
We chat awhile, then move on to pray.
Today her responses are immediate and clear.
As we make our way through the Our Father
I sense a presence in the space behind me.
Concentrating on the moment, I continue:
Lord I am not worthy that you should enter
Under my roof ... As she receives the host
A warm breath caresses the back of my neck.
Turning, I see an elderly resident in slippers
Her face stricken. A single sob escapes from her.
Placing a hand on her forehead I say the blessing.
Her full-on smile radiates down the length of my arm
Something is unlocked in us.

Nativity at Barkston Ash

Credit St Francis of Assisi
who started the whole thing off
with an Ox and a Donkey
borrowed from his friend Giovanni
at a cave near Greccio in twelve twenty three.

In this year's Nativity Play
the teller of the tale is a Robin,
who has got the news from a Dove,
and includes all the usual characters,
Shepherds and Sheep, Camels and Kings,

along with a flock of birds
of indeterminate identity,
and a cluster of stars
calling themselves The Milky Way.
The birds take their radar by the stars.

As they get near to Bethlehem, and see
the gifts of Gold, Frankincense and Myrrh,
they realise they should have brought a gift.
The three kings remind them they are birds.
They bring the gift of song.

And so they proceed to the stable
and there among the assembled cast
offer their gift to the baby boy,
an up tempo number called
We Found Jesus.

Prize for most original costume
goes to Joe, a Seabird, his
floppy yellow webbed feet
made from his mother's
rubber gloves.

Taking Flight
For Brendan and Sinead

The pale wafer of the moon
Is still definite in the lightening sky.
It perches on the top half of the windscreen
As I drive west towards the airport. Behind me
In the rear view mirror the sun is just rising.

I don't get up this early that often
But the flight is as the flight must.
Tomorrow I celebrate your Wedding Mass.
It is a good omen, the moon and the sun sharing
The same sky, one handing over to the other.

I hold this moment now as a memory.
I held it then as a promise, a blessing.
Long life. A graceful union. Finn.
He hadn't begun to happen yet, nor
Did we know that would be his name.

And now the news of twins
As you head back to Brisbane
Where the sun and the moon change places
And the water runs down the sink
In the opposite direction.

I give you what remains of the moon
And what hasn't happened yet of the sun.

Elijah

I

No rain. Not even dew-fall for half of seven years!
Ahab had not taken to my warning.
'Hide' God said. 'Go east.' So east I fled.

The Wadi beyond the Jordan was an unfamiliar place.
The Ravine at Cherith, a cutting deep in the rock.
I found a small space underneath an overhang.
That would be my hiding place and bed.

The river still ran, though everywhere around
the land was parched. After I drank my fill
I lay awhile in the water, cooled myself,
washed red dirt out of my beard.

The birds were strange to me. I did not know their songs.
When I saw the ravens I thought they'd come to steal
what little food I had, then pick my eyes out.
I scared them off with stones.

As darkness fell the movements started. Frogs, newts,
Fire salamanders creeping down the gorge to drink.
A huge blue-tongued lizard rubbed along my leg.
The water's murmur continued in my dreams.

In the morning the ravens came again. Then
the meaning of the promise dawned on me.
'The ravens will bring you bread and meat.'
Twice daily they fed me, as if I were their young.

During that first moon the flow of water waned.
By the third moon the river was completely dry.
I had no choice. I headed out for Zarephath.
That's when I set eyes on her.

II

She was dragging a tangle of sticks
with the child resting in her hammock.
I asked for water, then bolder for a little bread.

Her shoulders slooped, her eyes were empty.
This was a woman who was close to giving up.
A widow? I asked her. She told me yes.
Her husband? Killed in someone else's war.

She didn't speak his name. 'A good man' was all she said.
The child, when she put him down, was two years old.
He ran around babbling to himself, and laughing.
He pointed at me, reaching up to pull my beard.

Her home, down in a hollow among trees
had been luxurious once, but that was in the past.
Her last morsel of flour was almost dust.
A blue jug held the last few drops of oil.

'I'll make a meal of this, for you and for my son,
and after that we'll die.' As if having me die with them
made some sense. With her smooth long fingered hands
she kneaded that meagre little mound of dough.

She watched it rise, then handed me the scone.
She baked another one with what was left
and shared it with her son. She did this
not thinking of the next day or the next.

Her loss had taken her beyond smallness, beyond
the hoardings that grip us when we have too much.
She reached inside herself and kept on finding more.
The flour did not run out, nor did the oil run dry.

I grew fond of the widow, and I came to love the boy.
Time and time again that child drew us from despair.
She, seeped in sorrow, would let him pull her back.

The sickness came on him suddenly, he fell into a faint.
I saw her holding his limp body. Her voice cut through me:
'Man of God, did you come here to kill my son?'

His eyes were glazed. His lips went purple as
his breathing stopped. I took him in my arms
and went upstairs where the air was clear.
I prayed as I have never prayed before.

'O Lord let his breath come back. Let him live.'
I lay over him, trying to give him body heat,
three times. Three times I thought he'd gone.
At last the seizure left and he grew warm again.

The Lord had heard my cry. I gave him to her then.
She laid him down, asleep, then looked at me.
'Now I know you are a holy man of God.
The truth of God comes from your mouth.'

III

Fearing Jezebel I fled again, this time heading south.
From Beersheeba I went on alone
a day's journey into the desert.

I stopped beside a broom bush, its flowers
white with purple hearts. I sat there wanting to die.
My life seemed a long succession of failures.
I asked the Lord to take me.

I lay down to sleep, and in my dream I was awakened.
There was an angel who said I should get up and eat.
There was a cake of bread baking over hot stones.
There was a jug of water. I ate and drank.

The angel touched me a second time, saying
unless I ate the journey would be too long.
To this day I cannot tell whether the angel
came in my asleep or my awake.

All I know is, I lay down wanting to die
and I awoke restored resolute and strong.
I walked each day until noon, took shelter
from the desert heat, then walked on till late.

I took sustenance from the juice of berries.
Evenings I gathered sticks and made a fire.
I roasted morsels: edible roots, grubs,
once, a snake whose throat I'd cut.

You must remember I was no longer young.
At night the desert cold got in my bones.
Sometimes waking stiff, I'd stir the embers
then watch for falling stars until first light.

I reached Mount Horeb on the fortieth day.
I climbed slowly until I found the cave.
I thought of Moses then, and knew
I was on holy ground.

IV

The question nagged. What was I doing here?
The covenant had failed, the altars smashed,
and except for me, all the prophets dead!

'Go out and stand there on the mountain' God said.
There came a powerful wind. It keened and swooned.
It almost tore the mountain down. God had often come in wind
its grip and grind, but God was absent from that sound.

And then an earthquake came. The very mountain shook.
I'm not afraid of tumult. I like being in the thick of it.
I'd meet God on my own turf. But God was not
shaken loose in the shaking of the earth.

And after that a raging fire. I remember being on fire
in the days before my hair grew white. When the call
of God first fevered me I was a ball of flame.
But here in this fire, there was no sign of God.

Thunder, wind and fire had never frightened me.
But silence did. I went to the mouth of the cave
put my cloak about my face. I was afraid.
That's when God's whisper came.

Soft as the breeze, and gentler than a flower.
– no sound of waving tree, or beast or bird –
the deepest silence I have ever heard
and in that depth God spoke the quiet word.

No longer earthquake, wind and fire. Now
God would speak in the whisper of a lyre,
in ordinary things and ordinary speech.
This truth I now must learn and teach.

My prophesying days are done.
Three tasks are left. The final one:
Anoint a prophet who will do the same.
Elisha, son of Shapath is his name.

V

Looking down the valley, the air was
intimate with spring. Birdlife drew my eye
to the teams of oxen, their strength harnessed exactly.

The young ploughman schooled the leading pair.
One, an elder with the necessary slowness of gait,
the other young and raw, his strength not yet refined.
My approach when at last I made it was badly timed.

He saw me coming but before he recognised my purpose
I swung my cloak around his shoulders. It was too sudden.
First he'd have to finish ploughing, and then put in the seed.
He'd have to wait for harvest. He'd have to ask his parents.

Maybe that I took him by surprise was just as well.
A prophet's life is not for one too easily persuaded.
Even as he was recoiling from me I tried to put it right.
'You don't have to leave all this, unless you choose.'

I walked back up the hill to a sycamore grove and waited.
It was late afternoon when he came from his parent's house.
He told the workmen to unyoke the teams, take them home.
The young ox he took himself, slaughtered it on the spot.

He built a fire and turned his plough into a spit,
the workmen gathered round the tang of herbs
the smell and smoulder of the roasting meat.
They left the bones strewn along the headland.

The fire smouldered as the plough's hard wood
blistered into blackness. A soft glow embered
in the darkness. When at last he came walking
toward me, his gait was absolute.

Epilogue

It was clear that God would take him soon.
There were many rumours: Bethel! Jericho!
When he mentioned the Jordan, we were ready.

He wanted to go alone, but Elisha wouldn't hear of it.
In the end they went together. We watched him part
the waters with his cloak. We saw them walk across.
Then a storm blew up, enveloped them in whirls of dust.

A sirocco from the desert which didn't envelop us.
We could see their shapes filtering in and out,
heads close together talking, next thing blurred,
like ghosts of trees, or birds in flight. Suddenly

we saw it all, clear as moonlight: the horses
of heaven, ears pricked, eyes opened wide, flame
flaring from their nostrils in snorts of scorch and burn.
Their shod hooves were clustered sparks, their fetlocks

fine-boned streaks of light, their hocks a smooth
brown flame, their manes of yellow flowing fire.
Their bridles, the reins held tight, their collars of
matching purple bands tackled to a chariot of fire.

The carriage was a solid block of cobalt blue,
its doors a burning orange glow. The wheels
were spins of crimson, the shafts primrose pink.
When the storm cleared Elijah's cloak was lying

in the dust. Elisha tore his garment, placed the mantle
around himself, then headed back to us. Some insisted
on setting up a search. They scoured the hills, thinking
he'd been kidnapped, or that walking in a trance he'd fallen

down a cliff. Elisha let them, his mind was somewhere else.
Three days searching convinced them he was gone.
Now everywhere God's spirit is, Elijah lives.

Sleep Well

What you have to remember is to not look at the clock.
Whether it's nearly morning or just past midnight
you'll only get bogged down and begin to fret.
Did you turn off the gas? Did you lock
the garage door? Is the lawnmower safe?
You must cut the grass, and fix the fence,
which reminds you of the missing pliers.
On and on you twist and shift.
Another quick look and the hands
have barely moved. This goes on
all night, anxious snatches of sleep
in an invaded house.

❋

When you wake do not turn on the light,
you'll forget and look at the clock.
Go to the bathroom in the dark.
Flush the toilet then slide back into bed.
Listen to the water as it sings in the cistern.
Let its high notes lead you away
to snowdrops or the almost full moon.

As the sound dies, listen. Go to places
you have once been and want to be again.
The vineyard on a hillside near Macon.
The clean air above Grindlewald.

Or, tumble into the sea over the Great Barrier Reef,
glide into the waving coral, surface on the Pacific rim,
Vancouver Island, the hot springs and the black bear
that looks you straight in the eye and smiles.

Next thing you'll be a birch tree riding a saddled horse,
the wind in your leaves. You'll be ready to wake then.

A Better Place

You see it all now in slow motion.
The back-to-backs emptying. The houses
lonesome then derelict, the roofs coming off
and the walls groaning. You see the cobbled
streets un-cobble, and the fancy stone-faced
retaining wall grow higher and longer, and
below it the dual carriageway shaping out.

Heavy machinery clangs, and at weekends
sits there defiant. Then, on the Monday
Mrs Armstrong's house comes down.
Mrs Armstrong is in a better place
her daughter says, not meaning
that she's dead. Nor is her house.
It's still breathing, somewhere.

Meanwhile the new houses back on
to the park, and the stone-faced wall
is still sturdy though darkened by time.
Forty years, and the carriageway, last time
you drove it, had repair signs and machines.
Looks like they're widening it again. You wonder
what Mrs Armstrong makes of it now.

Wild Boar

I'm looking down the hill-field towards the brake.
I notice how in the north corner, the boggy part,
a figure appears, blurred at first then clearly visible.
Dark skin. Cloven feet. Bristly snout. Tusks.
His hind quarters are caked with mud.

And now I'm watching from a different angle.
Much closer. A second figure begins to emerge.
A quiet man wearing a brown suit, overweight.
His face fleshy, harmless, rounded into a smile.
He nods at me, then minds his own business.

Suddenly the boar rears up and turns on him
pummelling him with his front hoofs – which
have become fists – in a burst of explosive rage.
I watch helpless, grief stricken with regret.
I didn't know I could be this volatile.

In an effort to protect himself the man covers
his face with his arms deflecting the blows,
at the same time trying to reason with the boar.
Some vague message begins to filter through.
The velocity of the attack subsides and stops.

The man points over the ditch and beckons
the boar to follow him to some neutral place.
As they disappear I see the boar from the rear.
He's walking upright, wearing a check jacket.
His haunches are still caked with mud.

Spell

Almost
before dawn
can draw breath
daylight urges these
eerie lingering shadows
fly back into that lost light
go before the nearly morning
hides your last and longest flight

In Dante's dark wood you wait
Jacob-like you wrestle in the night
knowing how vague residues remain
lie ominous within the gathered flame
making through the open eyes of stones
no comforting or blind enlightened sounds
outliving the filtered fragments of your doubt

Prepare yourself to rise and face
quickened moments after sleep
resist a slim oblivious escape
slowly let the embers light
then float up like a kite
until you fully wake

Vexation stirs the early hours
waits without respite until
x-rayed by the shadows
your dark becomes a
zoom of light

Orbiting the Earth

How I got here doesn't matter now, I don't think
I was trying to escape. Hiding inside that little capsule
Was short-sighted, but deciding to leave via the blow hole
Was clever. Becoming a meteorite wasn't my intent.

So now I orbit the earth, anticlockwise, at sixty seven
Thousand miles per sec. Everything feels motionless
Travelling this fast. I can't tell whether I'm cold or hot.
Up here it's not about that.

There's not a puff of wind. I can feel it not blowing
On my face. No sound either, there's nothing to hear.
I've got a tickle in my ear I cannot attend to.
Every time I move my arms I go into a spin.

Rolled up in this foetal ball was fun at first.
I thought I'd go cheek by jowl with the stars,
Visit the Plough, meet Orion's daughter in her
White slippers, stay for breakfast and dinner.

In all this space there's not much room. I notice
How my toe nails aren't cut, last time I pared them
Was in Cuba. I think I've just seen Havana. I don't
Want to run into Fidel and not have my toenails right.

One small step! But that was the moon. I took
A big jump. Now I daren't stretch myself out
In case I elongate, and the kids down below
Call me names like O'Rory Borealis or Comet.

I go with the flow. I avoid cosmic rays.
Proton or Antiproton, I don't take sides.
I'm minding my molecules. I don't want
To be the cause of a change in the weather.

Aerodynamics

The sparrow darts
in flits and starts
quickly masters
flying arts.

The swallow swoops
in waves and hoops
catches midges
as she stoops.

The fulmar's flair:
to play with air
above the cliffs
as if in prayer.

With wide wingspan
the eagles' plan:
to rise and float
because he can.

And so I sift
and swerve and shift
to find the note
then let it lift.

Generation Gap

They know when to break a hole in your fence,
First when you're not looking, then when you are.
They'll work out when you're away on holidays,
And arrange for cider bottles and beer cans
To be in your garden when you get back

They don't have pets or grandmothers.
They never get toothaches or lose sleep.
They don't have a birthday, or bleed.
They only go to school on and off.
Their parents couldn't care less.

None of them will ever get a job.
They'll join the army to see the world,
Go around in boots and shoot foreigners.
After that they'll become debt collectors,
Or be part of an outfit for clamping cars.

You were never into anything like that.
When you were their age all there was
Was fat blokes who shouted after you,
Complained when you climbed their fence,
Threatened to report you to Connolly or Mac.

Bookshop

I spot him in Eason's on Patrick Street.
Pottering around with a stick. His shoulders
Hunched now, though he's wearing a good suit.
Scanning the shelves: Philosophy, Poetry, Politics.

Back then he was forever bursting out,
the knees and the arse of his trousers, elbows,
the stitching under his arms. He was well informed,
widely read, academically nearly always in the top one.

Married at nineteen, his six-foot-four frame
towered over her four-foot-ten. Last heard of in 67
when back from London. A boozer on Grand Parade.
'Drunk and disorderly,' the report in the Examiner said,

He could have been a professor or a lawyer,
a scientist or a judge. He never followed
his dreams as far as I know, but who is to say.
He moves ahead: Psychiatry, Psychology, Pyramids.

Canberra Sunrise

You wake to find blood on the pillow, your face
and lips crusted, the taste of blood in your mouth.
Alarmed, you jump out of bed. 'Only a nose bleed,'
the mirror says. You wash it off, then go outside.

You walk beside the plots of native grasses,
stand among the totem poles, hear the water
gurgling at the foot of the stainless steel cross.
Silence hangs from the leaves of the eucalyptus.

You drive out to the hill overlooking the city.
Parking at the Golf Club, you pass the sprinklers,
feel the moisture on your sandals. Four kangaroos
lie beside a bunker, a dozen congregate under trees.

They watch motionless as you come closer, then turn
and run. Bounding and gliding across three fairways
they wheel down the valley, coming to a stop inside
a pool of light. You watch them watch the sun come up.

Alaska

After we board the Arctic Explorer and sail out
On Resurrection Bay, after we look at the calving glaciers
And listen to their rumblings, after we watch the ice floes
Float past us only a few yards away, after we smile at Sea Otters
Cavorting on their backs with toes up, and admire the Walruses,
And the Stellar Sea Lion with his harem asleep on the rocks
Smooth and slippery like great globules of soap

The Captain calls our attention to the rich exotic bird life,
Naming the Tufted Puffin, the Double-crested Cormorant,
The Albatross, the Rhinoceros Auklet, Black-legged Kittiwake,
The Emperor Goose, then the magnificent Bald Eagles with
Their snowy feathered heads, their nine-foot wingspan,
As they rise and soar, higher and higher. 'This terrain,'
He confides in us, 'is an orthinologist's paradise.'

We drop anchor for lunch. He talks about habitats,
Mating rituals, endangered species. There was a word
You used back there, I say. Something about paradise.
'Orthinologist,' he offers, 'to do with birds and bird life.'
Might the word be Ornithologist, I innocently enquire.
'I don't think so,' he tells me. 'At least I hope not.
I've been using it for fifteen years.'

Pacific Rim

After seeing the black bear munch grass in the shadows
While her two small cubs play in the sun, you walk under
The green canopy of rainforest, lush in the clammy heat,
And sit on the great tree trunks that lie along the tideline,

Then take the boat ride from Tofino out on the Pacific Rim
To where the bald eagles nest: four tons of sticks and rubble
With the solitary bird sitting on her solitary egg while her mate
Shows his wingspan as he scans the skyline foraging for food.

Out here the dark waters gently heave. Further out the great
Factory ships swallow up multitudes of halibut and salmon.
The boat pulls in to a remote jetty and you follow the track
By the water's edge to where the hot springs are hidden.

You see steam rising, hear the water hiss, find the pool
Among the jagged rocks, immerse yourself to your neck,
Plunge into the ocean; immerse again, and again plunge
Until every muscle and sinew has let itself relax.

The young Japanese couple next to you know about Ireland.
They quote from Yeats and Heaney. Lying back the cold air
Caresses your face as you let your eyes linger on the horizon
Its wingspan stretching the four thousand miles to Tokyo.

Xi'an

After our encounter with the Emperor Qui Shi Huang's Army
Of Terracotta Warriors, we decide our next stop would be
For noodles. As we explore a warren of side-streets

A young woman in a doorway signals us to come inside.
We're in search of noodles, we tell her. 'I show you
The best noodles in Xi'an,' she says, 'and afterwards

You come to see my show.' She's as good as her word.
The noodles are out of this world. Thick, with a rich
Peppery taste that makes me want to sneeze.

She sits apart as we enjoy ourselves. Afterwards
She guides us through the maze of alleyways
Until we arrive again at her doorway.

She brings us upstairs, and shows us her array
Of watercolours on rice paper. Exotic plants,
and birds: a matching pair with blue wings,

Yellow beaks, black tails,
perched on an orchid-like tree
With red-and-white poppy flowers.

Another with dream birds, their heads green,
Their blood-red feathers going white at the breast,
And hiding in a tangle of dark green leaves.

Both hang in my sitting room now, next to
The calligraphy of Yeats: *We can make our minds
So like still water that beings gather about us.*

Last night I dreamed they had begun
To lay blue eggs of bone china, and when
They hatched, the room was lined with orange warriors.

The Jacket

Donegal Tweed, a thank you for my small mercies.
Reserved for big occasions. Aintree. The Gold Cup.
I loved the velvety insides, the texture of the lapels,
The one thing I thought might survive our demise.
But when I tried it on after your final coup de grâce
The chill of you was there in the sleeves.

Years later we patched things up, though we never
Got to the bottom of the rift. I held on to it thinking
We'll always have Paris, but I didn't wear it again.
I took it with me, wrapped in polythene, as I moved
From place to place. Things levelled out over time.
We tried to be civil whenever we met.

At certain moments some of the old warmth came back.
We've been fine for decades now, all that in the past.
I came across the jacket last week on an annual clear-out.
The speckled green is pristine, the lining smooth and cool.
The elbow patches and leather buttons rugged and strong,
And it still fits. But the shiver of your stare has clung on.

Afterwards

When Ed left the cloakroom and walked outside
the last person he wanted to run into was me.

If it was heaven's gate, he'd have turned back
if he had seen me first.

And now we have to walk the six hundred yards
to the flats, where we're both in residence.

Sensing his awkwardness only makes it worse.
Pretending not to notice makes it worse still.

He's angry as hell, and I don't have a bother.
I try small talk, but it's stilted and tense.

I ask the time of his basketball game.
He says it's been called off.

Has he anything lined up for the weekend?
He says he has not.

A jogger on the opposite side of the street
seems to offer a possible way out.

Ageing

I cannot reach the spoon, and trying to get it
with my foot only pushes it away. If I pull
the table out I'd be giving in. In the end
I get on my knees, only to find the damn thing
is still beyond my reach. And what comes to me: how
during those years at St Clare's, his constant niggling,
and the notes he put in my room on my day off: 'The lights
were left on in the Church again,' or 'The Sanctuary Lamp
has gone out,' taught me how to stand up for myself,
go on the offensive in ways I'm no longer proud of.
'You'll be old yourself one day,' he grumbled.
'And you won't be around to see it,' I retort.
I can hear him now, having the first laugh.

Inis Oirr

First, it was reading Seamus Heaney's poem
While crossing over from Galway on the Ferry:
The one about not embracing, embracing his father.
Then, it was seeing the headstone out on the rocks:
'In fond and loving memory of Joe Brown
11.05.1967 – 11.07.2009.

Thanks to the kind people of Inis Oirr
For their help, prayers, respect and dignity,
And the O Tuarisc Family for recovering Joe's body.
St Theresa pray for him and all those taken by the sea.'

And now, in the ruins of Teampall Naoimh Gobnait
A swell of tears surprises me. I have to steady myself.
What is it that draws me back here, year after year
To these barren rocks and tiny fields surrounded
By stones, not much bigger than a coffin or a pram?
What is it I have done and not done with my life?

The Stray

My hip is improving by the day. I can walk farther
and for longer, though I'm still using both crutches.
Here on the Stray on a Saturday afternoon in October
with the leaves in their glory, people are walking dogs,
others pushing prams, or taking a short-cut to the shops.
At the far end a group of kids are playing five-a-side,
and nearer an old man on a bench takes the autumn air.

But best of all is the line of four men with fishing rods,
complete with waders, bait, and the rest of the tackle.
A fifth man, also in waders and with an air of authority
watches them as they cast their lines and reel them in.
He's giving instructions: how to throw their arm back,
the correct angle of their elbow when making the cast.
I watch them for a good half hour before I head back

to St Roberts, imagining them imagining themselves
hip deep in a salmon stretch of some imaginary river,
or a loch teeming with trout somewhere in Scotland.
Which is all well and good, but fellas, will you listen,
you'd be better off sitting below in Betty's Tea Shop
for all the fish you'll catch on the Stray in Harrogate,
where even Jesus Himself couldn't conjure up a catch.

Taking a Fall

Sunday morning, just out of hospital, I sleep late.
Karen has put a rug by the shower, so my feet
won't have to touch the cold floor. Good idea.
Placing my crutches onto the rug! A bad idea,

and before I know it I'm gone Eddie the Eagle
flying downhill after the crutches. (See in slow-mo.)
A futile grip on the door handle doesn't help much
but does slow me a tad, until the door hinge cracks

and I'm off again. Then the second hinge gives way.
I land on the floor, on the only part of me that's myself,
my right hip and right shoulder. Left hip replaced last year.
Now both knees replaced. The landing is surprisingly soft.

And. Action. Now the door is coming to clobber me.
Heavy glass door and, naked, wet, badly shaken me.
The door comes to a halt three inches from my face
its corner caught on the top of the radiator. And. Cut.

I slither along the floor, get hold of the sink, raise myself.
This episode requires a period of extended meditation.
In the bedroom I sit on the bed and absorb the narrative.
When my father taught us to ride horses, falling off was

an important skill. ROWL he'd shout, after you'd lost your
balance and begun to slide. And you'd roll and hit the ground,
but you wouldn't hit it, you'd glide off it. I heard that shout
when I rolled my car over, off the M6 at Tebay, in 1989.

He'd died in 1971 but his voice came clear in the night air.
So figure this: I landed at right angles instead of straight out
and clattering my head on the radiator. Sitting here on the bed
the word ROWL reverberates again, his voice as clear as ever.

Holy Katie

She was famous for the number of Masses
she'd get to even on a weekday. On Sundays
it was easier. She'd go to first Mass at 7.00
and stay till the end of High Mass which began
at noon. That was six Masses and six sermons.
But on weekdays it meant finding out who was
home from the Missions and which one said Mass where.

'There's Fr Hegarty, he likes to say Mass
as early as 6.00. The poor man can't sleep, after
the doing he got that time in China. Then there's
the retired Bishop from Brazil, he comes in at 8.00,
and young Fr Tom home from Africa, the poor lad
gets tired quick, he can't get up of a morning
after catching a dose of that oul Malaria.

In August there'll be plenty more home
from England and America.' Katie could
fit in a rake of Masses no bother,
as long as she had her timing right.
From the Convent to the Pro-Cathedral
and back, and up to the Hospital chapel,
Eight minutes on her rickety bike.

She'd leave one Mass after Holy Communion
and get to the next before the end of the Gospel.
That way she'd clock up eight or nine on a good day.
One time she managed an even dozen.
Then there were the Holy Hours, Novenas,
Stations of the Cross, where she gained a score
of indulgences, several of them plenaries.

People joked about her. Being that holy
couldn't be good for you. But nobody ever
accused her of being a craw thumper.
Imagine my surprise years later, reading
about her in an English paper. How she
cornered a fox, how she killed him
with her bare hands.

Waking the Dead

Religion was not a problem except for funerals.
You couldn't go inside a Protestant Church
but you could go to the wake if there was one.
So, when old Mr Baker died, Catholic neighbours
made their way to his farm-house to wake the dead.

After shaking hands with the bereaved with the usual
'Sorry for your troubles,' they went to the room where
the corpse was laid out. They hesitated about praying,
not wanting to cause offence but unsure whether prayers
were any use. They complimented how well he looked.

After a while the young couple excused themselves
declaring they were going to bed. What to do next?
The dead couldn't be left alone at their own wake
regardless of their religion, and so it was agreed that
John Eugene and Denis Charley would stay the night.

They talked in low tones; local news, the price of cattle,
the end of rationing, and how the volunteers on the run
used to sleep here knowing full well the Black and Tans
wouldn't raid a Protestant house. Eventually talk ran out
and they sat in the candlelight letting the long night pass.

Hearing footsteps on the floorboards overhead, followed by
the metallic tinkle on the chamber pot, first his, then hers,
the two men took it in turns to go out to the fuchsia hedge
to relieve themselves, to look up at the Plough and admire
the vastness of the heavens; and then resumed their vigil.

When the boards creaked again late-on accompanied
by the acoustics of the chamber pot they walked outside.
A narrow band of light was appearing over Derryclough,
'That was one quare wake,' John Eugene commented.
'It was,' Denis Charley said. 'All pissin and no drinkin.'

Chapel of Rest

Mrs Delaney, who had never smoked in her whole life
lying there in the coffin, with a cigarette in her mouth.
A rag week prank is one thing, this was beyond a joke.
Everyone barring the deceased was reeling with shock.

The O'Connors were livid. Profound apologies given
to Mister Delaney, his four daughters and three sons.
In all the years, going back to eighteen eighty seven
nothing remotely like this had happened to them.

They were family friendly, the chapel in Blarney Street
left open for the next of kin to visit whenever they wished,
was their proudest boast. This would never happen again.
But it did, the very next week, and the one after that.

Every effort to catch the culprit came to a dead end.
Their biggest worry was word spreading in student
watering holes like the Wash or the Courthouse Bar,
or God forbid, showing up in the Examiner or Echo.

It was old Mr O'Connor came up with the plan.
The next Thursday, – it was always on a Thursday –
he put on his funeral suit, lay down in the coffin,
had them powder his face until he was chalk white.

He lay there for a good hour or more and not a stir.
The wood got harder. He had cramp in his left foot.
Hearing a noise he took a deep breath. Next thing
he felt the filtered tip probing his lips. The prankster

creeping back out thought he heard a noise. Turning
he saw the corpse sitting bolt upright, the cigarette
held up. Last thing he heard before he hit the floor
was a hoarse whisper: 'can you give us a light.'

Coal Tit

When I get back to my room after breakfast
I see her fluttering about among the furniture.
My coming disturbs her at first, but gradually
she quietens down and perches on the speaker.
As we watch each other I talk soothingly, bird talk,
easy as wind, or a branch hidden in a cluster of leaves.
'Thank you bird for giving me this St Francis moment:

While I was praying in the chapel you came to pray
in my room.' I edge closer, pretending I'm not there.
She sees through me and switches to the mantelpiece.
There she bobs along, taking it all in: the fat candle,
the empty flower vase, the photograph of my mother,
then makes a sudden whoosh for the half open window.

The force of the impact, her beak and head on the glass
does for her. I pick up the ruffled ball of feathers
hold it in my palm, watch the glazed eyes close.
I feel her body go rigid, her little legs stick out.
I place her on the window sill, then take her
in my hand again and wait for her to expire.

After a bird eternity, ever so slowly, though
I can't be certain yet, life comes back into her.
Heat, a fluttering of her eyes, a shake of her head.
She has only knocked herself out. She lies still
on her side warming my hand, and after a time
gets to her feet, her tiny claws gripping my palm.

She looks at me, neither of us saying a word.
For a good five minutes my hand is her friend.
In the end, when she's ready, she flits away.
I see her disappear among the rhododendrons.

From the Middle Gate

The first gate was for letting the cattle out,
The cows' gate we called it. And then there was
The iron-gate, which opened into the northern field.
But the middle gate was where our father
And his father looked from on a Sunday, after
Having the dinner and after walking the land.

From there they could look at each field, watch
The river on its twisty way past the inches, until it
Disappeared from view by Johnny Noonan's cottage.
Today William Kingston farms both sides of the river.
His herd of Friesians, a few hundred in number
Spread out like jigsaw pieces in black and white.

Back then a herd was less than twenty, of mixed breed.
Shorthorns mainly with the odd Hereford or Kerry cow,
And a straggle of calves and heifers. Back then
The eye-line was decorated with furze and fuchsia
Along with Ash, Rowan, and Elm trees,
Or copses of evergreens beside a farmhouse.

Telegraph poles started the change in 1956
Bringing us electricity. Followed a decade later
By the poles that carried the telephone lines.
Now, from the middle gate there are Wind Farms
Waving their arms above the line of hills
To the northwest, the northeast, and east.

Seven so far; though to the south and southwest
The horizon is still clear. Jim Carty's house
Is where it always was. Cyril, D.J.
And Dan Collins: their houses are long gone.
But the place-names still carry the old music.
Mileenawillian. Derrylugga. Inchinagotagh.

In the Garden

Yesterday in the garden I noticed my father
Walking next to me. We were easy
In each other's company, now
We're both in our seventies.

I was thinking of us in our twenties,
There was no sign of his arthritis.
'You did a good thing,' I said, meaning the Flying Column,
The part he played during the troubles.

How dangerous it was in those times in these familiar fields,
The dug-out in the Gravel Mountáin, Carraig A Thonnaig.
'That took a lot of courage,' I said.
I'd never told him this before.

'You did a few good things yourself,' he replied.
I was very pleased to hear it coming from him.
'You mean the poetry?' I asked.
'That too,' he said.

Remembering the way he had with words,
How he'd sit at the table to write an important letter,
Rehearse it before my mother, try it one way
Then another, before writing it down,

'It was you passed it on,' I said.
'Do you think so?' he asked.
That's all that happened between us.
Next thing he wasn't there again.

Found

In an old handbag
At the bottom of the wooden chest
Where she kept her very private things:
The homily I preached at my First Mass.
My sister's ponytail, cut when she was twelve.
The yellowed newspaper account of the inquest,
And, folded in its faded green cover, his copybook.
James Mac Carthy   English

October 18 – 1949
There is one armchir in my parluer.
I have not a donkey at home.

November 29 – 1949
My father has a lot of turf.
My mother lights the lamp.
It is grand to get a Christmas card.

December 6th – 1949
Everybody has a soul.
The sole of my shoe is not broken.
Daddy Christmas brings nice presents.

January 1950
I write with a pen.
I have black shoes.
The road is hard.

The Bright Room

As I enter the bright room I see in the vase
The orb of my face formed into a fish
Gliding among the stems of tulips.

Finely shaped from the small shell of myself
I become a frail hand of feathers, I become
A red candle in the yellow sky.

My eyes are led along the length of the lintel
To the floating ark of Archimedes
To the delicate ship of heaven.

Deirdre of the Sorrows returns my look.
Being gazed-upon I am sucked
Into the blue of her eyes.

I take off my shoes, feel the floor
Float out from the thin harbour
Of my unremembered self.

Under the pale rainbow
I am carried without resistance
Down the drag of disappearing night.

I have said this before, but don't remember.
I have walked along the parallel lines of light.
I have arrived at daybreak and am no longer blind.